Gana: Where's the baby?

Tom: I don't know.
Is she in the cave?

Ugga: She isn't in her bed.
Tom: Is she behind
the dressing table?
Ugga: Dressing table?
Tom: Yes, there! Look!

Ugga: No, she isn't behind the dressing table. Where is she?

Tom: Look, there's something under the carpet.

Ugga: The carpet?

Tom: Yes. Look there!

Ugga: Oh yes! There she is!

Tom: It's all right, Mrs Gana.
The baby's in the bedroom.

Gana: The bedroom?

Ugga: Here's the baby, mum.
Gana: Oh dear!
She's very untidy!
Tom: Who's that?
Gronk: It's the teacher.
Come on.
Tom: The teacher?
School? Oh, no!

Tom: Is this your school?
Ugga: No, it isn't!
It's the baby's school.
Gronk: Goodbye! Be good!

Gronk: Look! This is our school.

Ugga: Do you like it?

Tom: What a funny school! Where are the tables and chairs?

Ugga: Tables and chairs?

Teacher: What's this?

Ugga: It's a boy!

Gronk: He's my friend.
His name's Tom.

Tom: Good morning.

Teacher: Good morning.

Zonk: Hallo, Tom!
You can sit here,
behind me.

Tom: Where's my book?

Ugga: Here, Tom.

Tom: Ooooof!
Thanks very much, Ugga.
What an enormous book!
What a funny school!

Teacher: Please draw a picture.
Draw the tiger.

Tom: Draw the tiger?
Oh dear.
I don't like this school.

Zonk: Tom! Draw the tiger!

Teacher: What colour is the tiger?
Zonk: It's orange.
Ugga: No, it's yellow.
Tom: No, it's yellow and black!
And it's enormous!

11

Teacher: That's a good picture.

Ugga: Where's Tom?

Gronk: He's behind the tree.

Tom: Help!

Zonk: Ha, ha!
Look at Tom!

Tom: Oh! The tiger!

Teacher: Run! Goodbye!

Gronk: Do you like our school, Tom?

Tom: No, I don't.

Gronk: Come on.
Let's go home.

Gronk: Hallo, mum and dad!

Tom: Oh no! It's a tiger.
Help!

Gana: A tiger?
Where?

Gom: No. It isn't a tiger.
It's a picture on the wall.

Ugga: It's a good picture, dad.
Gom: Do you like tigers, Tom?
Tom: No, I don't.

Illustrations by **Simon Stern** Design by **Barry Cooper** ISBN 0-86158-322-1
First published 1983.

MGP Mary Glasgow Publications Limited, 140 Kensington Church Street, London W8 4BN
Printed in England